5inALife

How To Help Your
CHILDREN
Build Communication
CONFIDENCE
5 Minutes At A Time

5inALife

WARREN D HAYWARD

5inALife

How To Help Your
CHILDREN
Build Communication
CONFIDENCE
5 Minutes At A Time

WARREN D. HAYWARD

5inALife
*"How to help your children build communication
confidence five minutes at a time"*

Copyright © 2020 by Warren D. Hayward

ISBN: 978-0-6488654-0-7 PDF
ISBN: 978-0-6488654-1-4 EPUB
ISBN: 978-0-6488654-2-1 MOBI

Illustrations: Copyright © 2020 by Erin Bortoluzzi
Cover Design: Warren D. Hayward & Joanna Zhang

For more information,
email 5inalifeway@gmail.com

FIRST EDITION

www.5inalife.com

Table of Contents

A Personal Message..vi

Flourishing Seed...ix

5inALife Way...xv

    Chapter 1 You Are Where You're
From and You're From Where You Are..............1

    Chapter 2 Habits of Positivity...........................9

    Chapter 3 Their Choice, Their Story..............15

    Chapter 4 Sharing Is Caring:
Share What You Do..19

    Value of Money..24

    Abundance...25

    Celebrate Together...29

    Tradition and Gifts...31

    Chapter 5 Investment of Tomorrows:
Wrap It Up With Love.....................................35

    Wrap It Up With Love.....................................40

    Messages From My Children...........................51

    A Mother's View..54

Dedication..57

Notes..59

A Personal Message

We all have our own story of life's opportunities, growth, dreams, realities, aspirations, self lies, failings, public and private wins. I live a blessed life, full of culture, traditions, family, friends, career changes and entrepreneurial adventures. Not all completely positive, though great in terms of the life lessons and defense armory that I quietly carry with me, shielding the negativity this world often exposes.

As a father and leader across many life disciplines, I understand the challenge of helping our children and younger loved ones develop into confident people. Confidence is everything.

The family represents many things and it's what I care most about, starting firstly with my own family and how I can be a positive role model within it. Through positive examples, I strive to influence the people I connect with and empower them to be positive role models in their families, especially for their younger members.

This book was conceived over six years ago however the first word was typed 17th November 2019. Writing is part of my everyday corporate life via emails, presentations and conveying a message. This project was a completely different form of writing and personally emotional. The emergence of memories I thought I'd lost. The proud realisation of hope I still have from an early age and my passion to instill hope in my children.

This writing process only became easier when I took the focus away from myself and the need to sound like an author. I wasn't an author writing this book. I reminded myself to simply serve as a messenger of the 5inALife idea. It's much like public speaking, the best speakers take the focus away from themselves, know their subject well and convey their message with pride and visible belief for what the information will provide for their audience.

This is the quintessential me, the prospect of helping people that I love fulfil their goals brings me serious joy.

This book is the formal exposure of a simple idea that you, yes you, can implement into your homes and communities, with little investment, creating a safe environment for the growth of confident people in future generations.

Warren Hayward

5inALife

Flourishing Seed

I am the seed of my parents, my late mother Enid Hayward and fit father Dudley Hayward.

I am proud to be the big brother to Darren and Gerard.

My parents and I were born in Durban, South Africa, and we moved to Perth, Western Australia, in 1977. My brother Darren was born in Perth and then we moved to Sydney, New South Wales, in 1979 where my brother Gerard was born. My parents: two people sowing three male seeds.

I've briefly described three locations where I lived. In Chapter 1, the emphasis will be on appreciating where a person lives at any point of their life and their surroundings, without forgetting where they came from. At this point, I'd like to share a big reason for how we came to be in Australia and the relativity to my family's journey, the seeds that have spawned from the decision to leave South Africa including the flourishing seeds that live in my home today.

I enjoy the escapism of movies, whether in bed with my wife and kids at home or at the movies on the big screen with the scent of popcorn and comfort of cinema seating. Some movies stay with you forever, maybe not the names of the key roles or locations but the concept and undertone. *Sliding Doors* is one compelling concept I think of frequently. The movie depicts two parallel timelines of Gwyneth Paltrow's character Helen as she makes the train after getting fired from her executive role and the story that unfolds versus Helen missing the train after being fired and the different story that unfolds. I'm not a fan of spoilers so I'll prevent sharing the movie further to help you enjoy the escapism.

The concept of choice or circumstance, "sliding doors", plays out many times in our lives without us realising it. It's like the Choose Your Own Adventure books I used to enjoy as a child, where you get to a chapter end and can decide which path to take and eventually your story will end in a manner of multiple-choice decisions. This is life, choice or circumstance then progress.

Our family's major sliding doors moment came through tragedy. My mother is the eldest of 10 siblings, my father, the second eldest son of 8 siblings. Big families were common in those times.

Life in South Africa in the era of apartheid was of course particularly challenging though families adapted and attempted to fulfil their own goals. Moving abroad for better pastures was spoken of and sometimes pursued but to no avail due to lack of overseas sponsorship, fear of the unknown or other reasons. My mother and father also spoke of life abroad but with no serious attempt.

During a farewell celebration of my dad's Uncle

and Aunt moving to Australia, unfortunately, some persistent gatecrashers were allowed to enter the party under duress. After some time, they were asked to leave and things escalated, resulting in my dad's brother Alexander being fatally stabbed and the gatecrashers getting away.

My dad and his brother Alexander were remarkably close, working together as apprentices and socializing as young men. My father being the younger brother only had revenge in mind at all costs. Though my mother also hurting, coupled with the vision of what their life could equate to should her husband make the biggest mistake of their young family's life, made some quick brave decisions. I was two years old at the time. Her quick decisions and foresight resulted in applying for Australian residency without my dad's complete knowledge. Fortunately, as my dad is a builder, Australia had a strong need for builders and we were quickly accepted into Australia after a short few months since the tragic death of Alex.

Leaving South Africa with the family still in mourning was a difficult moment in time and I can only imagine the quiet sad moments shared by my parents in a new country with no immediate family in Australia. My parents had some cousins and friends in Perth hence our settling there, and June 1978 presented the joy of a new family member, my brother Darren Michael Hayward. The birth date of Darren was also a day of sadness as my dad's father Michael was buried after a short and sudden illness. My father had the guilt of not going back to South Africa to see his dad's last moments as he did not want to miss the birth of his second child.

We stayed in Perth long enough to host my mother's parents and my father's mother on holidays which gave them a taste of our new life. My mum's parents also visited Sydney to see my grandfather's brother and family with the encouragement of a great future in Australia. Returning to South Africa from holiday, my mum's parents would share the opportunities of Australia and possibilities for their children. Sydney soon became home for us in 1980 when my parents decided to drive across from Perth to Sydney for better employment prospects. With communication via international telephone calls on a regular basis, the South African family gained more hope for relocation to Australia and during the course of eight years, 1977 to 1985, my mum's parents and all her siblings migrated to Australia where we all still live. Unfortunately, my dad's siblings and families didn't join us in Australia. They continue to pursue happiness and spiritual paths whilst the family seeds continued to grow in South Africa.

Sliding doors. My beautiful and nurturing mother passed away in March 2012 and during the funeral service of several hundred families and friends, I spoke of the tragic death of Alexander and how had that not happened, where would most of the funeral guests be at that point in time. I spoke of my aunts and uncles and my first cousins here in Australia, many of which are now married to other nationalities and have children of their own. I spoke of my Australian born brothers

Darren & Gerard married respectively to Australian and Maltese background wives and their children. I spoke of course about my own life with my beautiful wife Geraldine, born in Mauritius and the four children we have. We used to joke and call our children "Africians", a blend of African and Mauritian children. Sliding doors. I would be lost without my soulmate Geraldine and our beautiful confident children and all of this may not have happened without the courage and visionary leadership of my mother and the love my father had for her and me to leave South Africa and slide away from likely conflict.

5inALife

5inALife Way

Sometimes the simplest things in life produce the biggest impact.

5inALife is the method of asking your children to present a topic of their choice and present that topic for five minutes at least once a week in a method of their choice. This presentation is delivered in front of the rest of the family members, preferably at the same time every week, for example, Monday night at 8 pm.

It must be a topic that the child chooses relatively to their current life. It could be a movie review, book review, school project, their latest sports game, a story from class, a friend's party or anything of their choice.

Let's think about communication choices. When you are having a conversation with a friend of a topic you understand and have a deep connection to, you are at your most vocal and speak with confidence and passion. This is why you must allow your children to choose their topic each week. You can influence and provide ideas but you should not choose the subject for them. Not knowing the topic also adds to the experience of receiving the information with enthusiasm, making you a good recipient of the presentation, a good audience.

Five minutes sounds long and may be difficult in

the first few weeks, though your children will surprise you with their ability to adapt and fill the space with information and substance. Various methods of delivery should also be encouraged such as using photos, props, computer presentation tools such as Microsoft PowerPoint or Prezi or Google Slides and a timer should be used to ensure the five minutes is adhered to, with a four-minute warning.

Every presentation must start with an introduction.: "Hi, my name is Warren Hayward and today's 5inALife is on…"

The introduction helps set the child into a presentation sharing mode with a style and tone that best suits the topic. The introduction must also be visibly checked with eye contact with each and every audience member. A greeting of "eyes." The child ensures you are paying attention without distractions. This greeting of "eyes" throughout the presentation is encouraged and used as feedback after the presentation if you noticed your child looking away or down at their feet. You'll begin to see various levels of energy exuded with each different topic as your child starts to build character and alignment to the topics each week.

Most literature will highlight that communication is a blend of words, tone of voice and body language. You may be surprised that body language is the most important when it comes to the listener or audience understanding the communicator. The tone of voice is the next weighted measure with words being the least important to understanding the message. Posture will also grow with 5inALife presentations and you'll notice your child appear taller simply by the confident stance.

Another important element is to help your children eliminate "ums" and "ahs." Every time they say "um" or "ah," we, the audience, should repeat "um" or "ah." Not only will the child find better choices instead of "um" or "ah," but the audience will become active listeners making the process a collaborative learning moment. Soon, you too as parents will start to be reminded of your "um" and "ahs" from your children, which will help you, too, become a confident communicator.

Many books have been written about the investment of deliberate consistent practice. The benefits of hours and hours invested in the accomplishment of something you are passionate about. Regardless of what the passionate topic is, whether it's sport, business, academics or public speaking for example.

What we don't see is the many hours and hours of investment that goes into being truly good at something. Deliberate consistent practice closely monitored by a caring coach or caring critic forms that magic of confidence and belief of being better. The Beatles and Ed Sheeran had hundreds of hours of shows before they had commercial success. Michael Jordan, David Beckham, Manny Pacquiao and the many more sporting greats who have invested hundreds of hours of deliberate and consistent practice in the chosen passionate sporting platforms. The interesting thing about the same sporting examples above is that these same people have invested the same attitude and passion in fine-tuning the communication-related careers beyond sport.

There's no magic number of hours that will flick the switch to being great but rather the cumulative and consistent effort towards confidence and then greatness.

Practicing is only half the challenge and there's certainly an argument to a magic number of hours of practice with examples such as genetics, timing, luck, wealth and/or resources amongst the arguments. Practice isn't a sufficient condition for success. I could play basketball for 100 years for example, but I'll never play in the NBA.

I am a firm believer in the merit of deliberate consistent practice and the thousands of hours of football I have practiced in my time, enjoying the practice more than the 90-minute football games. The great thing is, I have been fortunate to have great coaches guiding my growth and I played at a competitive level with maybe some luck, timing and resources which may have improved my semi-professional success. I genuinely wanted a professional life in football though it was not to be. Nevertheless, the hours of deliberate consistent practice formed good habits of ball mastery, a vision of the game, touch and technique. Good habits of the game I still possess now though not at the same pace or stamina.

I also have thousands of hours of DJing to my investment of time which has allowed me to enjoy DJ entertainment business success and income for my family that has exceeded 25 years. That DJ income has allowed my wife and I have the choice to have her fulfil the most important role in the world, being a great gorgeous mum and not needing a conventional job.

Had I not invested that time in those two passions of mine, football and music, I would not have met many positive people in my life. I attribute countless positive outcomes including my employment career, football coaching success and teaching many DJ's to create DJ businesses of their own. This collective attained success for myself and others has derived from hours of deliberate and consistent practice in subject matters than truly matter to me.

This is the heart of the growth: I was passionate about things in my life that matter to me and therefore I applied the hours.

5inALife will grow your children's character towards those tens of hours of presentations in a deliberate, consistent and safe manner, allowing them to express their thoughts and learnings with confidence.

Every opportunity to increase that presentation confidence will produce magic in your children's eyes. Most importantly you're making time for them and our presence is the greatest present for our kids.

I appreciate that my wife and I have shared this vision for communication confidence for our children and every family has different circumstances. Some families are single parent families and some parents have mentally or physically challenged children. Some homes have multiple families within and some homes have one child and one parent. I stand with these various family cultures though this philosophy is still suitable for your home.

I want to be respectful of the parents out there that have struggled with internal relationships, addictions, illness and employment challenges. I pray your situations are temporary in nature and you can use this book as a fresh start in your home towards a future change of health, wealth and happiness and good fortune.

Investing time with your children, the next generation of your family tree, is so important.

The five-minute presentation is the foundation of the 5inAlife philosophy. I'll share in all chapters many other opportunities to capture five-minute moments with your children. Enjoy!

Chapter 1

YOU ARE WHERE YOU'RE FROM AND YOU'RE FROM WHERE YOU ARE

We Australians are so blessed to live in a beautiful country where diversity and culture are recognised and alive. The 2016 Australian census revealed just over six million families call Australia home. Of people surveyed, 34.4 percent had both parents born overseas, highlighting the diversity that thrives in our communities.

I remember being a minority as a black child growing up around mainly white children which certainly involved plenty of bullying and conflict. Most of the time I had the confidence to deal with it via verbal retaliation or wit, however sometimes it was a physical response that was the outcome, something I'm not proud of but we learn.

In hindsight, this was probably my South Africa heritage, the culture struggles and confusion I was trying to accept and naivety or immaturity among the community at large.

The language and dialogue you hear as a child within your circle of family and friends play a major part in your future identity. I've witnessed family members and friends, really good people, talk ill of another race in a particular subject matter, however, I've learned that it's generations of change that will change this language for our children's children starting as soon as possible. I've likely made poor language choices at times, similar to my family members, however I'm more conscious of it based on many years of corporate management life with principle-centred diverse inclusive organisations.

Through experiences in many areas of your life you develop a backpack of communication styles. Through awareness of your children's early backpack, they will be better equipped to live a confident communication life, regardless of where you're from and where you live, present and future.

A great place to capture five minute moments, build communication confidence and opinion is the dinner table wherever you are.

The dinner table is where we learn between bites.

Family togetherness at the dinner table, gazing into familiar faces we love, we reflect on the day's events and share possible disappointments. At the dinner table we raise our glasses to school accomplishments and career milestones. At the dinner table we dream, we ponder, we laugh, tell jokes and chase sarcasm. At the dinner table we plan holidays and birthdays, we wonder where the time went and discuss memories of previous years. Together at the dinner table we learn the lessons that family generations teach such as manners, values, contribution, cooperation, respect, communication and self-love.

I personally have fond memories of my childhood dinner moments with my mother, father and brothers sharing stories of the day and mostly laughter. Laughter felt like a sixth member of the dining table as my mum, heavily outnumbered, held us boys down with her humour and charm. The dining table was a great meeting place and my parents had an open dialogue about all sorts of topics, especially since my father never missed reading the daily newspaper and often shared findings from it and wanted our thoughts on various topics. My mum was a great cook and with four hungry males each night to serve we never missed coming to the table, regardless of what we were playing outside, down the road or river, when mum called dinner, we came running to "live between bites" and eat together.

Vision. What a powerful word, used in many references. We see vision daily as we live in our diverse world. We see the vision when we recall beautiful memories and some people have a vision of the future yet to be realised. My parents, in search of buying their first home, found an old shack on a large block set on top of a hill. I was seven years old, Darren was three and Gerard was born two weeks after we moved into "the shack" in Emu Heights, 1982. A fibro house, two bedrooms, one living room, a kitchen and a disconnected back room with laundry. We had been to inspect the house prior to the purchase. Darren and I were convinced the old lady owner was a witch with her big indoor dogs, the large front yard full of trees and growth. We were convinced she was hiding her secrets on top of that hill, it was visibly scary to us boys.

My parents clearly saw something very different than us boys and their vision, a new house with huge plans for the future and now three boys to fill the home with laughter was a bright vivid future. It wasn't long before that vision turned into reality as my dad quickly got to work painting and stripping old dog urine scented carpets. The sense of achievement made a huge difference to our home and we were happy. My brothers and I shared a room for many years and it created a bond that is still so strong today. The vision made way to further home renovation plans, massive plans involving the excavation of large portions of land in front of the house, turning a slope into twin double storey, double brick buildings separated by a steep set of stairs and balcony. The excavated clay trenches were dug out by many families and friends "hands," achieved on weekends, and it was my earliest memories of seeing a project team working successfully towards a common goal.

Of course, the renovations continued for years. A builder's house is never quite finished.

We have countless memories of living on stilts, propping the house up during excavations. We lived without windows, walls and water some days. We lived with makeshift driveways and played around chopped down trees and railway sleepers but the eventual home transition would reveal the vision.

Dad was drawn to the large yard for his "boys" and boy did we take advantage of that as it morphed into a football field, then to a BMX racing track with moulded dirt ramps and, yes, a basketball ring with a homemade backboard against a tree. We had so much fun and freedom outdoors in that yard and I can only smile just thinking about it.

So much sacrifice was made by my parents and it's only on reflection in adult years that I truly appreciate what they achieved from such humble beginnings.

Mum and Dad were working parents, especially to finish the many house projects and still fulfil our weekend football travels around Sydney.

Dad would leave most days very early to go to work. Mum would call me into her room most mornings to remind me of my chores and ensure I didn't miss the bus. It's amazing the layers a woman achieves in morning preparation for work, both facial and garment layers. Mum could multitask with ease, advise me of important school matters whilst applying lipstick smudge-free.

One day, in particular, was hilarious. Mum went through the normal morning messages in my half-awake state, slowly placing the various layers on, ready to present her immaculate self to her place of employment. Mum would drive to Emu Plains Railway Station, park the car, then rush to make the train platform most days. But this morning, she felt a little more breezy than usual and it wasn't the lower Blue Mountains air.

Before long, mum had returned home laughing the kookaburras away and as she came back to her room, I, of course, following her to find out what happened, she picked up the newly pressed dress she had forgotten to put on. For her undergarment slip caused many men to notice her that day and all she could laugh about is that she thankfully realised before getting on the train. This story was a belly laugh that dinner night and quickly swelled to the rest of the family and friends. Many others would probably have kept that embarrassment to themselves, not my mum, she was comfortable to share her mistakes and make them a treasured moment.

Memories of vulnerability and silly mistakes we can laugh about, build character into relationships and it's so powerful between child and parent. I know my relationship with my parents grew stronger as we grew in life experiences, not necessarily age. I worked with my father from a young age and saw how difficult life was. We would experience all sorts of building site challenges and accidents, most of which we could laugh over and frankly wouldn't be allowed in today's work, health and safety regulations. My mother worked with me in several businesses my wife and I owned, and she too saw how difficult these businesses were in a very different era. A sound and lighting retail business was foreign to my mum and it was certainly funny the day I had to explain the difference between male and female audio cables. But boy did we laugh a lot and experience many business wins and losses.

These memories create the foundation of "You are where you're from and you're from where you are." Our dinner table was filled with these stories and I truly hope your home too will be filled with stories that your children recall in their future. Allow your children time to contribute their five minutes at the dinner table without cutting them off. Watch them light up as they speak of fun or important stories of their own. Be 100 percent present with where you are, together as a family.

Chapter **2**

HABITS OF POSITIVITY

The nightly news is rarely positive. For this reason, my wife and I have rarely watched the daily news with our children. My wife and I have made conscious decisions to shield our children from the negative daily rhetoric that sells papers and TV time slots. This has been our choice, though I'm not opposed to parents watching the news with their kids. The challenge as parents is you need to find balance mechanisms to highlight to your children that the world is not all negative. There's so much hope and happiness daily though it seldom makes headlines.

This leads to important roles as parents in creating a positive environment of growth for our homes. Creating this positive environment impacts all tenants of the home including yourself and the younger minds yet to realise their potential.

Habits both positive and negative, simple or complex are formed over time and it's not easy to break a habit cycle or form new habits. Researching the internet will show an often consistent magic number of 21 days to break or form a habit with some smaller research studies indicating a longer range to truly lock in a habit. Regardless of the time frame, my challenge to you is to be intentional of what habits you wish for your children to bear witness to and start immediately, then let time take care of timeline growth just like we let time take care of height changes in our children.

If your child hears aggressive language, swearing and verbal abuse between mum and dad and their friends, it's not difficult to imagine the child growing up with these habits, too.

If your child hears appropriate praise and appropriate discipline for their conduct, it's understandable for appropriate habits to be formed to either create praise moments or minimise discipline. The challenge is, children are immature and it will take time for habits to form though we are the role models who should set that tone. Our children see and hear everything and very quickly form behaviours that are aligned to their surroundings.

5inALife will form part of that positive environment, a chance for children to express themselves with topics of their interests or topics which they want us to learn.

Imparting and exchanging information is the essence of communication. This information sharing is not always the case, especially when there are large differences in age, experience and interest. This is the classic situation between child and parent. It requires a conscious effort to be an empathic communicator, let alone a confident communicator.

The problem mostly appears due to differences in perception. An empathetic existence is our children trying to understand this busy crazy world and parents' perception of their children not growing up fast enough. Seeking to understand this world is very much a part of children's development and we too must recognise this within our parent-to-child conversations.

I want you to be cognizant of the differences in ages from you and your child or children and, to this point, further appreciate the differences in personalities that will exist in your growing home. My wife and I have different habits, different temperaments and personalities. We also have a different way of expressing emotions, especially love. Firstly, we have a different way of expressing love as partners, then expressing love as a parent team, and, of course, expressing love individually to our children.

Once we understand each other's expression and receipt of love, this forms greater relationships with our partnership. This is true of learning our children's expression and receipt of love and serving that emotion well for the greater bond of that individual relationship.

Our four children all have different temperaments, personalities and expressions of love which we need to be cognizant of when building this positive environment for us all to exist in and provide feedback through life. It's not one size fits all.

Feedback after 5inALife presentations is an important element to your child's confidence. As leaders, we need to give this feedback as a gift to their communication growth. For example, our son Quincy and daughter Bailey went through separate phases of constantly using the word *literally* amongst friends and conversations until we had to make them consciously aware of how much they used this word and encouraged them to discover alternatives. This was important and time-sensitive feedback as they thought it was pretty cool to use this interesting word and yes it was *cool* at first until it became a negative habit which needed adjustment. Because of their different love languages, we ultimately had to handle the encouragement in different ways for each of them to best suit their growth.

Words used well will help form character and 5inALife will become a great vehicle for children to discover and try new words in their presentations. Our leadership role is to encourage this positive word discovery habit.

Nonwords such as *um* and *ah* are a habit we unintentionally increase into adulthood unless we are made aware of how much we use them. Making your child aware of these during 5inALife presentations will create a positive opportunity for your children to discover different ways of replacing an *um* or *ah* with a time to pause and think, gather thought intentions and then complete the sentence or thoughts. This process of the audience repeating *um* or *ahs* during a presentation, as long as it's done in a fun way, will encourage new behaviours not only during presentations but also in general conversations.

Although I've done countless presentations as a business leader, I too need feedback on my nonwords. Recently my daughter Bailey was present during a 45-minute information session I conducted and after the presentation, Bailey said, "Wow Dad that was very good considering how long you spoke but I counted how many *ums* you said and I lost count after 100!" I was shocked, to say the least, but simply believed her and used it as feedback which is always a 'gift' for the next presentation I did.

This is an opportune time to highlight that I firmly believe in the 5inALife philosophy and the positive improvements it will make to our children's communication confidence, but it will not create perfect people and I don't pretend to be anywhere near perfect due to this ideal. I believe in being an everyday student and therefore we constantly learn from all connections and collaborations from all ages. My daughter reminded me of that when she comfortably shared my nonword discrepancy. I'm also reminded of this when seeking formal feedback from my colleagues and subordinates during formal and informal reviews, assimilations and roundtable sessions to help me better serve my teams as a leader.

If you are not seeking these opportunities to grow, you limit your chance to increase your value and if you limit your chance of increasing value, you shouldn't expect to earn more in professional life. Adapting to various temperaments, personalities, diverse backgrounds, ages, sexual orientation and experiences are part of life here in diverse Australia and not much different around the globe.

5inALife creates positive moments of increasing your children's value of time and audience appreciation, delivering content in a confident way where feedback is appreciated and yearned. They already yearn for our time and value. When our time and value comes with applause and pride each week, they'll find it easier to accept the gifts of feedback from us, their parents, their fan club and grow in confidence with every 5inALife.

Chapter 3

THEIR CHOICE, THEIR STORY

Growing up in this large extended family, there are many names to remember and personalities to accept. I remember warning my wife, girlfriend at the time, that there will be many people so don't feel overwhelmed by all the names, many conversations happening at once and stories you'll hear. Geraldine's character is confidently strong and since she could talk to anyone, it was a somewhat simple "getting to know the family" experience. Our children have grown up with events, Riley, our firstborn, experiencing her first party two days after her birth, straight from the hospital to a big family Christmas Eve.

As Riley and her siblings have grown, before many family events, Geraldine and I during dinner would run through the uncles' and aunts' names and associated children to ensure our kids felt comfortable to communicate and know the connections. I'll be honest that this connection challenge still exists today as the family grows in depth and we see each other so infrequently.

Yes, these large family events present the challenge of not being able to talk to all members and not all members being able to talk to you. Understanding this challenge leads to these name reminder games over dinner but it also leads to the importance of early confidence. So many age differences, so many personalities, so little time.

We encourage our children that if an adult aunt or uncle or family friend came to you to ask "how are you?", we as parents would be disappointed to hear one-word monotone responses like "good" or "fine" or "okay." We would highlight to our kids that these adults could be talking to anyone in the room and if they've chosen to speak with you, please give them more of whom you are, what you're doing at school or sport or what you're reading or a movie you've seen lately. Five minutes of sharing was the basic message. Simply be comfortable to open up.

We wanted our family or friends to get a sense of our children as unique individuals with different personalities and interests, not just the children of Warren and Geraldine. At the same time, the children would learn the art of conversation, a two-way conversation where a person is interested in what another has to say, interacting openly across topics, regardless of age.

Having these proactive connection sessions before events will help your children feel comfortable in the next big event whether it be a work function, family reunion or sporting event. Making them feel comfortable sets them up for communication success. Making them comfortable energizes confidence.

Conversations, especially from adults to children, tend to be open ended. For example, "Hi Riley, what have you been up to?"

Riley, therefore, has the opportunity to share whatever she wishes to share. Her choice, her story.

I'm sure you can agree, we feel most comfortable when we are talking about subjects we are genuinely interested in or passionate about.

Their choice, their story is also about proclaiming unique hobbies and interests. These hobbies and interests will evolve and adapt over time. Different fads will be introduced to the home during 5inALife and will help you get to know your kids so much more. You'll get to embrace Disney movies and their easter eggs, K-Pop artists, memes, TikToks, video games, latest dance moves, anime and many more topics that will surprise and delight you.

Special note: if any of the above do not sound familiar, it's definitely time you started 5inALife.

Chapter 4

SHARING IS CARING:
SHARE WHAT YOU DO

The dinner table is an important 5inALife moment in your family life. I encourage you to share with your children your own stories and lifespan of obstacles you endure.

My children have always known that I'm a supply chain professional and an expert at making systems, people and processes work more efficiently to get the right product to the right place at the right time and at the right cost. That's what I'm paid to do. In the past, I've shared with them basic supply chain ideals of moving a product from point "A" to point "Z" and the many points that are touched along the journey. Maybe it was boring or exciting to them but I felt it was important for them to understand why I go to work each day and also how important supply chain is— without it we wouldn't have all the physical items that surround us. Unless we start 3D printing everything or "beam up" *Star Trek-style,* the supply chain will always have an important role to play in society.

Back at the dinner table, I've shared with my wife and kids, for example, stories of hiring staff and the various questions we may ask during an interview. This led to giving my kids random interviews over dinner, not to say they were on the verge of employment but just to give them some daily life lessons combined with fun at the table. It was always interesting to hear their authentic responses especially when they try to answer as if they were an adult. Answering in front of everyone also provided invaluable response muscle when it was time to be interviewed in real circumstances.

Yes, articulate responses are valuable but equal to vocabulary, posture and body language are so important. Being proud of the way you look, the clothes you wear and the way you smell all play a valuable part in exuding confidence. This will sound odd to most people but ensure your children know how to provide a firm handshake. Deliberate and consistent practice shaking your children's hands so your sons and daughters understand that handshakes form a special connection to confidence and ability. There's an energy that breathes confidence from a firm handshake as opposed to sloppy fingers going through a greeting motion.

I appreciate that the world post Covid-19 may change its view on shaking another person's hand, however I believe a firm respectful handshake has guided my years well and I've warmly shared this view with my children.

Let's pray that successful vaccines can prevent Covid-19 and any other future virus outbreaks, and that appropriate personal cleanliness measures continuing to be instilled will allow for the handshake gesture to remain.

I recall when my son Quincy decided he didn't want to play football anymore. He had previously played at division one club level and was very competitive, however, he went through a traumatic experience just before finishing his final year of primary school. This experience left him in a wheelchair and at Westmead Children's Hospital for a month. It was a difficult time for our family as the doctors could not determine what caused this debilitation. Eventually, the doctors decided to increase pain medication and aqua rehabilitation sessions to get him walking again. He was released from the hospital and my wife dedicated her time to get to as many aqua sessions as possible until he gained the strength to walk again. My wife was amazing during this period and I still feel guilty that I didn't devote as much time to Quincy's care whilst I was climbing that corporate ladder.

Quincy gave up football that season and delicately returned the following year to many people's amazement. Though he had a good season, his passion for football wasn't there and decided not to return for under 13's. He said to me, "Dad, I think I'll find a job instead." Though my wife and I told him it will be hard to find a job at 13, during his first day of looking, Quincy landed a job with a newsagency which he would serve for 3 years. His dinner table interview gave him the confidence to comfortably speak to the newsagent owner, shake his hand firmly and get the job instantly. He started two days later.

Quincy's newfound part-time job also gave his older sister confidence and it was not long before Riley had her first job interview and she too got the job from her first interview. The importance of a firm handshake was evident for Riley too. After finishing school Riley moved swiftly into her chosen career of early childhood education and received full-time employment from her first interview. Quincy has since finished school and started university studying medical science and mechatronic engineering. I'm proud of Riley and Quincy as they confidently discover themselves, engaging with many other individuals of all ages. Their stories will continue.

One common trait we share in the family is the love of creativity: from art to comics, poetry, books, movies, TV and especially music.

Geraldine and I have had the experience of working on TV advertisements and extras jobs and we encouraged this for our children. Quincy has been the only child not yet to experience a paid TV role because he frankly wasn't interested in it. Riley, Bailey and

Marley have all done multiple TV advertisements and extras work which have been great experiences for them to see what happens on the other side of the camera, including taking directions from other adults, meeting other people and experiencing earning money at an early age. They've worked on music videos, company ads for McDonald's, Google, Commonwealth Bank, Alliance Insurance, Western University "Deng Thiak Adut," AHM Insurance and more and even some TV shows' extras sets. Marley had a lead role as a Kiwi ninja in ABC's *Soul Mates*. Riley at age 6 had her first role on Australian recording artist Paulini's video clip "So Over You" through to extra roles 10 years later in BBC's *Top Of The Lake*. ' Bailey has recently signed as a teenage reporter on Channel 7's animal-focused, factual entertainment news show *News Of The Wild*. This will be a great opportunity for her if embraced with a learning appetite.

One of my habits is not expecting something of someone that I haven't done myself. Actively sharing is caring, however, we can never want it more for our kids or anyone for that matter, than they want it for themselves. Therefore on the TV extras front, a keen eye would see a dark bald guy in a few cricket scenes of Australian TV series *Packed to the Rafters* season one, episode two.

Speaking of humour which also created controversy in other countries, my wife Geraldine, daughter Riley and son Marley all appeared on the "You Never Lamb Alone " diversity-influenced advertisement campaign. With more than 6 million views across various mediums, it garnered praise for its positive light-hearted representation of diverse Australia. Although it was banned in certain countries, it won the 2016 TV Ad of the Year for Meat & Livestock Australia at the Mumbrella Awards.

Value of Money

Sharing the value of money with our children is one of our most important roles as parents if we truly want them to be better off than our generation, and there's no better way for them than earning money in real-world situations as soon as possible. They learn to appreciate the value of earning money and, in our children's circumstances, getting up early to go to a set, patiently waiting for directions then following instructions over and over again for a few hours while seeing the many people with different skills involved in producing film work. This produced great lessons for our kids and I encourage you to find a way to share the value of money and what it can bring rather than just saying yes to every purchase or outing request.

We've never given our children weekly pocket money yet they've always had the responsibility of contributing to household chores for the benefit of our home, a place we can all be comfortable within. Contribution to the family home and keeping the house homely and ready for any guests brings great responsibility to each member of the family; my children know their contribution roles very well even though the occasional argument will occur. I hope to one day come into their homes and find their kids contributing to a place to call home.

Work in many forms is part of all our lives. We've always shared career promotions and/or milestones with our children as a percentage increase, such as a 5 percent salary increase, and how and why we received the increase. I've had the opportunity to work in companies that are "feedback" centric meaning we proactively seek feedback to gain more awareness of our strengths and weaknesses. Performance reviews, 360-degree reviews, mentorship programs, staff assimilations, roundtables, one-up meetings, and cross-functional blind surveys have all contributed to my improvement as a valued employee. I've shared many of these reviews verbatim to my kids so they can see what people think of me outside of work and how I need to improve. For much of life we see their school report cards; why not share yours with them? As mentioned earlier, we cannot expect to earn more in any opportunity without giving more or making ourselves more valuable. Our children must understand this concept as early as possible.

Abundance

Our daily prayer before dinner is thanking God for our life of abundance, an abundance of health, an abundance of wealth and abundance of happiness. The concept of creating more than what we need so we can give more, has been shared with my children all their life and its core is this attainment of abundance. Doing the right things in all three areas of health, wealth and happiness for self and others will eventually allow us to share with others in need and this is our end game, to live in this life of abundance.

I'm sure if you were to poll my family—eat out or homemade meal? —they would choose a homemade meal! Through our Mauritian and South African heritage, many of the meals we make are from Indian cultures, basmati rice with curries and spices, lentils, beans, ginger, coriander, turmeric, chillies, etc. Adding our weekly gaps of Indian foods with our love of various pasta and sauces, yes, we'd much prefer to eat at home. Salads are included most days and rarely unfinished as Marley, our youngest son is our salad boy and won't see it go to waste. The right food coupled with exercise serves our abundance of a healthy ideal.

I make every effort to lead the fitness charge with a combination of running, walking, boxing and weights. My love of football still draws me to the world game and together with some long-term buddies, our team aptly named La Familia, we play summer six-a-side football. It's more of a kick and giggle, though our competitive juices still ripen through the tournament and I'm happy to say we won it in 2019.

My wife also loves walking our dogs daily as we encourage the active lifestyle of our kids.

We need the energy to be successful. Healthy meals and exercise is an important element for this success and it serves as an important element for your children's energy and confidence.

An abundance of wealth is the goal of collective financial, social, time and status wealth, as is making sure we are doing the right things for ourselves and the important relationships in our lives. This is certainly not an easy ideal to achieve and something that should take a lifetime. However, when done ethically well it will leave a legacy beyond our time. Ultimately an abundance of wealth is about the freedom to do what you want when you want with whom you want. Creating more time in our lives to donate time and money is our social responsibility.

It can start with coaching a local sporting team, creating meals for the poor or helping at your child's school, paying it forward for our community.

Yes, I understand these are challenging ideals of health and wealth although the easiest is happiness. Laughter and smiling every day is a choice. Smiling and laughter cost zero currency so why deprive ourselves and our children of this valuable resource? As a leader at work and at home I make every attempt to ensure a balance of seriousness and fun. We have objectives to meet and we will meet them together in an environment that promotes "good times." At home, I can be a big kid very quickly, even after a tough day at work. I actually miss the days of rolling around on the carpet wrestling with the kids, making block buildings, Lego or playing twister. Make the most of those early years of being a parent and it's okay to have five minute moments of childlike behaviour. Happiness is a beautiful emotion to experience— make sure it's many moments for your children.

Happiness is but a choice. Here's a prime example. Thursday 13th October 2016 was yet another learning and testing day. It was late afternoon, most colleagues had left the office for the day and I was completing a day course called *Crucial Conversations: Tools for Talking When Stakes are High,* a communication course adapted from the book of the same name written by authors Kerry Patterson, Joseph Grenny, Ron McMillan and Al Switzler. I had just completed the post-course survey with high regard and headed back to my desk to catch up on the days' emails. I was not long at my desk when I received a call from Human Resources. Ironically, I was about to embark on a crucial conversation. The organisation I served as a leader for over nine years no longer required the position I held and the position would be made redundant.

It was certainly an interesting moment in my life, my first redundancy. I truly enjoyed working with many colleagues in that company as we had been through challenging times, I knew I would miss them, and I still miss many of them. After the customary offerings in the Human Resources department, I calmly returned to my desk, grabbed my briefcase and decided that the emails could wait until tomorrow. It was my daughter's birthday that day and we had family coming over to celebrate. We had a great night with the family and the last crucial conversation was with my wife just before bed with the unique news of the day.

The next day was my last day in that company. Ultimately, it was the best thing for all stakeholders. The company was able to fulfill its strategic plans through my role redundancy, I started a new role seven days on and we booked a great family holiday a few months later. Further great events would occur over the next few months. I started a new business, further expanded my DJ business, bought an overseas property and started a new role in a great company that I still proudly serve. Happiness is but a positive choice!

Everything happens for a reason and we all have a purpose. Purpose suspends problems. We are all going to have challenges and sometimes even problems but if we stay true to our purpose, the problems will only be temporary.

Find what is important to your family values and share with your children these beliefs. Make the time to share successes and failures and don't be afraid to be vulnerable for your kids.

Sharing is caring. Through sharing these experiences with your children, 5inALife will enhance the experiences and bring them to light.

Celebrate Together

Celebrations big and small within the family should be treasured and remembered.

Celebrating small wins via 5inALife will add value to your relationship as parent and child. Finding opportunities and specific points to praise is an easy win after every 5inALife presentation.

"Bailey, I loved your excitement today about J-Pop and the knowledge you have for BTS, it's amazing how much practice time they spend to get their dance routines so tight, as you mentioned." Praise complete, with specific reasons and points.

Bailey walks away from that 5inALife knowing we understand the topic, small points of the topic and we know her excitement for the topic. Bailey knows we care.

A powerful metaphor is the Emotional Bank Account. Relationships built with a series of deposits and withdrawals. Simply explained, when we do good by another person, fulfilling commitments and showing care represents a deposit in that relationship emotional bank account. Letting someone down, not being trustworthy and causing harm to another person is a withdrawal from that emotional bank account. The idea is to make as many deposits as possible and build up a large emotional bank account within the relationship and when deposits with apologies are unfortunately required, the bank account is not affected long term.

5inALife is a perfect tool for creating moments of praise and deposits into our children's emotional bank account. When we are genuine in our praise for them, their confidence will lift with each presentation and the by-product is they'll want to do a better presentation each week with the added benefits of this confidence spilling over to their schoolwork, assignments and extracurricular activities.

The goal is to create a momentum of small celebrations throughout the house and build positive individual relationships within the home. Celebrations create a habit of reward and recognition in the home and there's no better pronunciation of celebration reward like the announcement of a holiday! We did many road trips as family holidays when our kids were younger, as we liked taking long drives with our kids coupled with its affordability.

"We're goin' on a holiday y'all," was the phrase I used for every holiday ignition.

The conversation during a drive can be so much fun, that is, while they're awake, which also leads to more 5inALife moments to bring out that communication confidence. Fun road trip games, singing and joking around contribute to a great holiday experience and in turn will produce great content to formal 5inALife child presentations.

Getting away together as a family is so important and should be a goal set every year whether it's a long weekend away, a cruise or overseas holiday. We should escape the pressures of work and school to enjoy each other's company outside normal surroundings.

Tradition and Gifts

Holidays can also represent family traditions, and my mother's family have fostered great traditions over the Christmas and New Year festive season that we sincerely look forward to each year.

To recap, my mother's parents had 10 children, all of whom are in Australia, and the majority of us share the holiday season together over the course of many events. Commencing from Christmas Eve, many of us go to Mass together and then congregate at a family member's house, and 2019 was our turn, when the children, big and small, received gifts from Santa and opened them enthusiastically. Christmas Day is a large festive feast in another family member's house, followed by games and dancing in the evening towards Boxing Day. Approximately 40 to 50 people in a house are common during this time and celebrations are prominent.

We recover until the annual themed New Year's party which starts at 9 pm through to the New Year's first sunrise. This is followed by brief sleep before uniting again at another family member's house for a BBQ lunch and annual paired darts tournament. The previous year's paired darts team winners remain partners so they can defend their crown whilst all other names are drawn from a hat by my grandmother. Sixteen teams battle it out, eliminating each other until a grand finale concludes the festive season.

Whilst some people miss the other celebrations due to other extended family commitments, nobody likes to miss the Darts Tournament with the potential of being a Champion and having their names engraved in the perpetual trophy. History was made in 2020 when my son Marley and partner Steve earned Champions status, both first-time finalist and Marley becoming the youngest winner at 12 years old. The champions provide a spontaneous speech to a packed emotional crowd and "We Are the Champions" is collectively sung for the neighbourhood to hear.

Celebrating together is a must in our children's lives and when combined with family tradition can only represent a positive impact on all affected lives.

Memorial moments beyond five minutes of ongoing reflection and laughter for years to come.

When you give a gift, doesn't it feel great when you know the recipient of that gift is truly thankful? As our children grow up, especially primary school, birthday parties are never-ending and you need to create a birthday budget to manage the costs each year. With this being said, bringing your children along to pick out the gifts can be a great experience for them. The innocence of anticipation—as your child hands over a gift and they cannot wait to see the expression of the recipient—is one you can never get tired of. Their excitement comes from being part of the celebration.

You may not be a member of a large extended family though we are members of school, church, social or sporting communities.

I encourage individuals to embrace group success. It's great for your own health, you get to meet new people with different stories and skills. You get to make a positive contribution to the community and you'll feel great.

Your involvement in the community also sends a message to your children that being a gift is just as important to give a gift.

My goal is to have 5inALife a thriving tradition in all homes which extends to enriching communities and society in general: a gift to many households.

Chapter 5

INVESTMENT OF TOMORROWS:
WRAP IT UP WITH LOVE

Lexico powered by Oxford English Dictionary lists the word "investment" as an act of devoting time, effort, or energy to a particular undertaking with the expectation of a worthwhile result.

No greater investment exists than our children and their future.

There are so many ways of investing in our children,

whether through school choices, extracurricular activities, the books they read, the movies you allow them to watch at the right ages, the friendships you personally maintain and many other conscious life decisions.

Another great investment of time with children is family board games, puzzles and card games. We have fond memories of board games with the family including Cashflow 101, Monopoly, Cluedo and Sorry, our most popular choices, and I can assure you that no one holds back when trying to be the champion of the night through fierce competition. I would like to say all board game sessions were tearless though this would be a lie. Emotions often get in the way but we've kept playing board games throughout as a family and these are mostly fun times.

Repetition is the mother of all learning. This phrase is so old, it's actually a Latin proverb: *Repetitio est mater studiorum.* The Romans used this philosophy in a physical education program towards mastery.

There are many life lessons learned during family board games and repetition. Where games include money and decision making, this can set the tone for future real-life scenarios and influence future views about money and risk. As a family, investment ideals can be formed, character can be built and most of all fun can be attained.

I've personally used the games in corporate teams to help their family and individual goals. My reward is hearing my colleagues personally share stories of debt reduction through increased payments and completing loans early or investment attainment or growing a shares portfolio. I genuinely have joy for their growth as they make small incremental steps towards their personal goals.

No greater investment is our children and their future. Playing these fun board games with an educational element plants small investment seeds into children's minds and you'll see these seeds bear fruit in future choices.

Renowned U.S. neurosurgeon Dr. Ben Carson has a remarkable story of rapid life confidence stemming from the investment of his poor but resilient mother. Single mother Sonya raised her two boys Ben and Curtis via two to three jobs simultaneously in Detroit and when the boys started to struggle at school she made massive routine changes in their life. One such change involved limiting TV time and replacing that time with reading. Sonya required the boys to read two library books each week and provide her with written reports on the books, even though she could barely read them, due to her own poor education. Sonya had her boys believe that anything is possible and soon the boys began to enjoy reading and writing the reports and this process improved the academic results too, ultimately improving their confidence to excel in their chosen career paths.

When we commit to a higher level of anything whether it means sports, music, art, academia, the level of consistency must also step up and I encourage your homes to lock in 5inALife consistently once a week. If only done during school periods, your child will achieve between 30 and 40 presentations per year, over 2.5 hours of quality time with the family listening intently to every presented word. I also encourage the use of video recording each presentation and building a library of confidence progression and future sharing.

This investment, without any money, could just reap massive rewards for your children's future if done well. It could also reap massive rewards for society's future as we need our children to develop and innovate for the future beginning with personal confidence and art of communication.

My wife and I are proud of our children's development, but are they perfect? No way and neither are we as parents. The principles and values, however, are instilled in timely moments with the help of our extended families and communities, whilst we have recognised early that we must be "response" able and willing to invest time where needed.

Parenting is not easy and I'm still learning. That learning discovery begins at their birth. The best advice we received and shared is never let your children develop the habit of sleeping in your bed. As tempting as it is to feed your child in bed and then allow them to fall asleep with you, I passionately advise you to stop yourself.

Feed them separately from your bed, wrap them gently in the cot and build the early independence. You'll thank me for this one as you hear of the many stories of children still creeping into mummy and daddy's bed in their teens. This deliberate decision is a powerful form of investment for you and your child.

It will add value to their confidence-building journey too and provide a smooth transition to 5inALife as early as possible.

Our daughter Riley, has a beautiful soul, much like my mum. When she was about 4 years old, she loved to give us imaginative dance routines in our bedroom before bed. Riley was so cute as she pranced around the large carpeted dance floor rolling around at times and extending her fingers with contemporary flair. We would clap for her final pose and she would wander off proudly to sleep.

Riley also loved to sing and tell us all sorts of stories, however, she had a lisp which was also so cute at the time. Knowing the potential future challenges that lisp could bring, we quickly enrolled her into speech therapy sessions which soon eliminated the lisp. These are the investments into their futures.

Riley and Quincy are 18 months apart, whilst we also went through the pain of a miscarriage prior to Quincy's conception. Mainly due to business ventures and over-ambitious decisions, we had a five-year gap before Bailey was born. Bailey and Marley are only 15 months apart. We always wanted a big family though it was never about the cost of maintaining a big family, it was the time required to have a big family. Team Geraldine and I have always known our key roles, myself the workaholic and big thinker, Geraldine the nurturer and events planner. We've made so much sacrifice for our children over the years and will be proud when all four children have completed high school.

The investments of parenting time continue to be applied, and I have no doubt that Bailey and Marley will take advantage of opportunities in their final years of school whilst navigating the opportunities outside of school. They simply need to make themselves proud, love themselves, invest time into their talents and as my Grandfather used to say, "may their challenges be small."

Wrap It Up With Love

The world is evolving at a rapid speed due to technology enhancements and social engagement with the technology, but we too must evolve, make serious plans for our future, our children's children's future and how we want to leverage our talents and our time. Influence starts at home with schools and society on the second tier of the education path. We as parents are partners with our school teachers, our sports coaches, our dance instructors, our music tutors, our family and friends, however the "village" that raises our kids starts with our influence. There are certainly great role models that children can aspire to be like or better than but we need to be their main sounding board and cheerleader. We must be the people that understand them, their personality, their attitude in the morning and night, their uniqueness and abundant talents yet to be flourished.

Influencer is such a buzz word in business circles today. Be that influencer in your home. When influence is served well, the likes of Michael Jordan,

Oprah Winfrey, Warren Buffet, Alicia Keys and many more successful people simply cater to your children's individual interests and technical inspiration combined with your family values.

We need to wrap this nurturing of a positive future with love in an environment which belongs to them. We need to consciously fill their emotional bank accounts with love and attention and promptly recognise when they are not fulfilling their potential. Tough love is needed at times.

I grew up during a period where our parents learned to discipline their kids from their parents which meant punishment by belt or stick. During this same time, the school system I grew up within also had serious discipline with the use of straps and canes. Most parents including my own and most teachers including the ones I respectfully remember used these methods sparingly. In the process we learned to respect our elders and the lessons they were trying to help us comprehend. We do not need to go back to physical discipline times by any means, however we do need to recognise when our children are not fulfilling their potential and correct them swiftly. This could mean minimising video games and TV time similar to Sonya Carson or encouraging more deliberate practice time in their passionate sport or art love. It could mean minimising bad influences in their lives and encouraging better behaviour and better attitudes.

We protected them when they didn't know how to cross a busy road with the basic rules of looking right, then left, then right again. And we had to remind them of these important rules many many times before they understood it and checked both sides instinctively. Continue to protect them by checking their communication language, posture and attitude choice. Allow them to check your language, posture and attitude too.

Over the last few years a post on LinkedIn, Facebook and Instagram has surfaced on several occasions titled as the '10 Things That Require Zero Talent.' They include:

1. Being on time
2. Work ethic
3. Effort
4. Body language
5. Energy
6. Attitude
7. Passion
8. Being coachable
9. Doing extra
10. Be prepared

It looks like a list that is being designed for schoolchildren but sadly this is directed to working adults. The need to write such a list stemmed from a rise in poor performers and had they simply improved in these basic items, they would achieve better outcomes. The list even managed to influence *Time Magazine* author Tom Gimbel to write a response claiming it's a total myth that these things require zero talent. They all need to be learned at some stage is Mr. Gimbel's view.

Regardless of whether you agree with the zero talent notion or top 10, I believe we as parents can influence our children to greater outcomes through the 5inALife journey. If we start from school age, we can create more than 30 hours of 5inALife presentations during the course of their school journey which can influence many areas of the "top 10 things" above and ultimately help them become engaging members of society, excelling in their chosen careers.

My opinion is the "top 10 things" list derived from adults not having a strong enough reason "why."

"Why" work at all…?

Likely to pay bills or to go on holidays or have nice "things."

The corporate world has countless examples of leaders taking charge with strong vision, mission, value and principle statements serving their company products and services. These statements are visible on posters and company collateral to remind staff, stakeholders and customers their intention and direction.

These companies start with "why" they exist and build from there, eventually through leverage of loyal employees aligned to the mission.

As per the "10 Things That Require Zero Talent," it's not as easy to find loyalty when employees don't know their "why."

Great businesses should ask tough questions of themselves and their strategy. Why are we pursuing this new hire, product launch or business acquisition in the first place and why will we complete this endeavour regardless of how challenging it may prove.

I have been blessed to work in strong companies that understand these principles. I have also had the good fortune to work directly with managers that provided great examples of investing time with their children as much as possible, being great leaders at work and at home. These people still actively engage in quality family time and when I catch up with them every few months, guess what we still speak of with passion? Yes, our children and their success.

Over the years I've shared my 5inALife practise with them with the encouragement to trial it in their home. Many of these past and present colleagues still use it today to great effect.

Good people, start with "why."

Let's start with "why" and transfer that focus to the most important organisation in your life, the one sitting around your dinner table each night. Find your why and help your children to establish their "why" too. Relative to their chosen professions one day, our children start to form their "why" in their late teens although sometimes tragedy matures these decisions too fast.

The passing of my mother at age 61 in 2012 redefined my ambition and inspired me to greater learning and leadership at home and career. It urged me to start and complete my MBA, double down on external investment growth and especially refocus internal investment growth at home. It also affected my wife and children greatly. They lost an inspiring influence in their life and I knew I needed to step up and love them more on behalf of my mum too.

Tragedy brought us to Australia and love influenced so many decisions.

Any influence you wish to place within your children's life will not be possible without a meaningful relationship with them wrapped in love. Five minutes at a time. Value attained in your relationship with them cannot be fulfilled without your own personal shift in attitude and a higher "end" in mind.

Wrap your own life with love, love from a partner, love from quality investments of time in meaningful endeavours. Make time for God in your life and understand your own God-given talents and purpose. The most important conversations we have are the ones we silently have with ourselves. God provides that anchor in my life to deal with the challenges presented. If it's not the same God for you, I respect that though I also understand a spiritual existence is part of your life whether you recognise it or not and the best way to find that is through love.

Our children will undoubtedly create some stress in our lives, whether it's through poor decision making, social pressures, society influences, adolescence, early ambition and many other factors. Most of the time we cannot control their thinking because we are all unique. What we can control is our action and reaction to their decisions and growth. Realise that change will inevitably happen several times through the course of growing up for you and them. Embrace the changes. Welcome change into your home; change often means growth.

The miracle of birth and the miracle of individual growth will be beautiful experiences.

I truly love seeing people succeed and love to see parents' pride in their children.

Thank you, Lord, for helping me create 5inALife. I gift it to the parents of future confident society members.

I am a proud father to four great personalities, named after music icons Riley, Quincy, Bailey and Marley. I love my roles in life as a husband, father, business owner, corporate leader, DJ, investor, football coach, Manchester United fan and now an author. I am a business professional with high ethics, strong leadership, and an investment mindset with a healthy balance of fitness and fun. An extensive career with many multinational companies across multiple industries and personal entrepreneurial adventures has afforded me a wealth of experience to inspire my children. I am an MBA graduate, yet I still have so much learning to achieve. I'm not afraid to share that vulnerability and humbleness with my wife, my kids and my circle of influence.

I have failed countless times for many reasons such as procrastination, time, money, over-ambition, naivety and poor timing among the many reasons and excuses I can make for the level of success or lack of success attained.

Be that as it may, my failure experiences have guided growth and overcome so many pressure moments in my career, I'm thankful to my wise friend "failure." Failure doesn't need to be the foe of success but merely a companion on the road map towards success that has a diminishing thought with each experience.

Failure is always possible and should be considered a wise option if there's a lesson to be learned.

When I was a teenager playing representative football, my dear mum used to drive all over Sydney looking for the playing fields. This is during the time of using a thick heavy street directory and not the GPS we have come to rely on these days. Rep football was strict, be there an hour before kickoff or you're likely to be benched. We were late many times early in the season due to failure to read the literal road map though we learnt from those experiences by allowing more time on future trips and taking in the landmarks for certain locations.

The road map of our children's journey will inevitably have countless moments that appear at first to be failings. I say "embrace it, learn from it, create improved goals from it and let it fuel our future celebrations."

I continue to have the pleasure of watching my children develop and adapt, serve their communities through academic achievement and representative honours in sports, debating, public speaking, music, dance, chess, religious leadership, school council and I'm sure many more in the future. 5inALife was just part of the process in helping them understand themselves, build relationships within the home and in their communities and give them a dash of personal confidence their futures greatly need.

There are fewer "fine," "good," or "OK" responses

in our house as we've learned to share more of what we are and what we want for our lives. My joy will be hearing your home also eliminate these one-word responses. I welcome stories of your children's growth and success to inspire others to use 5inALife.

Wealth is a measure of family attainment. The love of my children and future grandchildren and their children are the backbone to true legacy.

Your personal responsibility is to invest quality time with individuals and content that will add value to your life. This value will manifest prosperous dividends into your children's lives. Readers are leaders: encourage your children to find the content they will enjoy to read and then potentially present during a 5inALife book summary. Remember the content should be their choice.

5inALife will grow in quality with every meaningful session and build communication confidence five minutes at a time for your children. I wish you prosperity and passion as you grow with your children with laughter, learning and love.

Messages From My Children

"5inALife has helped me gain more confidence when speaking with others of all ages. I have become more aware about how I speak with my family members, colleagues at work and even with other families, as I work in childcare. I don't like public speaking at all, even in front of family, so 5inALife has challenged me to come out of my shell to talk about anything at all for five minutes."

Riley Hayward

"5inALife was an interesting experience growing up. Although I already had the confidence to speak publicly due to past experience in my leadership and debating endeavours, 5inALife provided a constant way in which to improve upon this skill in a simple yet effective manner. The manner of talking about a subject you are interested in or have experience in provides a passionate form of communication allowing for an easy experience in learning to express one's thoughts into a clear and cohesive matter publicly. Building confidence in a friendly environment allows this skill to be almost unconsciously used in daily conversation and public speaking activities. I believe the practice of this ability at an early age is imperative in developing confidence in yourself and in speaking to others especially for those who have social anxiety and those with the drive to lead others. Overall, I believe it was a positive experiment with the potential to grow and improve others who are not only in the need to build confidence but also those wishing to enhance their ability to converse with others. This is of great importance and need in today's society."

Quincy Hayward

"Growing up, I was never afraid to start a conversation and was very extroverted. I found it a challenge to express myself, make sense and elaborate my vocabulary from simplistic words. It annoyed me when conversations were limited by three-word answers. When on my hand, I was all babble. It wasn't until I learned through 5inALife to extend myself and how to converse. I was able to avoid ums and ahs and click my fingers to try and find the word I'm looking for. Not only was I able to learn how to make myself clear, but through the words of my siblings and parents, the body language, words and characters of others expressed through 5inALife.

Often, my siblings would talk about pieces of writings and work they did during school. From my own classes and the discovery of what life will be like when I too would be a high school student, I took an interest in extensive and descriptive writing. I developed a love of reading and learning, often when my topics in 5inALife shifted from talking about my favourite Disney movies to a book review and really long explanations on books such as Morris Glietzman's Once series. I found myself delving into the lyrics of songs, analysing how the artist would write, to eventually learn how to write my own songs too. In recent years, public speaking and slam poetry came to light which I became obsessed with, taking school opportunities in "Voice Of Youth" and debating teams to public speaking competitions where I progressed to the grand finals in 2018 and 2019.

Although I could say that it was through my own willpower that I became the extroverted, confident person I am today, I would be lying if I didn't say most of my influence was from the simple living room presentations I progressed from weekly. A lot of my success has stemmed through this five minute conception and is something I highly suggest beneficial for kids my age."

Bailey Hayward

Ever since I was a little kid, 5inALife has helped me have the ability to communicate well in school with my peers and teachers and in my everyday life. I am now constantly talking with my family and friends on different platforms of communication. 5inALife has not only taught me how to communicate better, it has also improved my confidence when speaking to a group of people or even with new people that I meet. Thanks to the key five minutes I had everyday with my family, I can open up and talk about whatever I want to with them.

Marley Hayward

A Mother's View

A good life is a collection of happy moments through photos, holidays and family gatherings.

5inALife has enhanced our children's ability to communicate as well as express themselves in a way which allows them to feel confident. They have grown tall, in a manner of walking through a forest and coming out taller than the trees. They can converse with those of any age, without feeling less than or inferior because of their age. They have learned to inhale their confidence and exhale any doubt, which will always carry them through life.

We live in a household with six different personalities, and 5inALife has glued us together no matter the differences, which has helped our family flourish by having greater communication. This communication is expressed in a way that our children are able to be themselves for any matter in their lives. The input, we as adults, instill in our children in their very young years will shape them into the adult they will become one day therefore making it the most important part of their journey in this lifetime.

We have one life to live and making the most of every moment with our children is vital in them knowing that they were loved by the simple moments of their favourite 5inALife topic which brought out the magic in them.

The most gratifying moment as a parent is to sit in awe and say, "Our family just shared a PRESENT moment in time."

May your family collection be all your hearts' desires and more.

Geraldine Hayward

Dedication

This message is dedicated to my mum, Enid Hayward.

My parents had a plaque at home that read, "I am the boss of this house and I have my wife's permission to say so." My dad and brothers know how true that was!

In loving memory of her sacrifice and love for her family.
Cancer stole you from us too early, Mum, but your seeds are still flourishing.

Gone too soon Mum, we miss you.

This book is also dedicated to my dad, Dudley Hayward.

I carry your high work standards and commitment every day.

Teaching my brothers and I love was evident throughout our lives, in the way you loved our mum.

Notes
5inALife Way

Chapter 1
https://quickstats.censusdata.abs.gov.au/census_services/
getproduct/census/2016/quickstat/036#cultural
(retrieved 14th December 2019)

Chapter 4
Patterson, Kerry, Joseph Grenny, Ron McMillan and
Al Switzler, Crucial Conversations; Tools for Talking
When Stakes Are High. New York: McGraw-Hill, 16
September 2001.

https://www.dandad.org/awards/professional/2017/
integrated-collaborative/25994/you-never-lamb-
alone/ (retrieved 17th January 2020)

https://www.theland.com.au/story/4770059/mla-
lamb-ad-wins-for-third-year-running-video/
(retrieved 17th January 2020)

Chapter 6
https://www.lexico.com/definition/investment
(retrieved 8th February 2020)

www.ingramcontent.com/pod-product-compliance
Lightning Source LLC
Chambersburg PA
CBHW071840020426
42331CB00007B/1795